CORRUPTION

CORRUPTION

New Findings From Neuroscience to Understand
Corrupt Behavior and Neuroethics

DR CYNTHIA CASTRO

MISIÓN

MISIÓN

Corruption
Published by Editorial Misión

Copyright © 2023 BY Cynthia Castro

ISBN: 978-1-958677-08-7

TO MIRYAM PATRICIA VILLARROEL de CASTRO: my mother, my source of inspiration for true justice, for her example of passion for the truth

TO LUIS ENRIQUE RYBIER: my great teacher, endearing professor, and best friend, for his example of discipline and intellectual honesty.

CONTENTS

PRELUDE

It was March 2014.

I was in front of the Jal Mahal, in Jaipur, India.

I fell into a deep sleep.

I dream that the Floating Palace was swallowed by the Man Sagar Lake.

When refloating, the rooms lit up little by little, one by one.

Suddenly, the palace goes inside my head and it lights up. The little lights were similar to Christmas bulbs. When I wanted to touch a light bulb, everything would light up, one by one, as if dancing to the sound of music.

I knew I was dreaming, but it was so real!

When I peeked into the palace of my mind, I could

see constellations, which would light up only if I peeked out and watched. It was as if the universe —mental— came to life, and its little lamps turned on only if I observed them.

I kept dreaming a lot more and, when I woke up, did so with the infinite sensation in my chest of having lived the experience of a cosmic and luminous dance, in which the stage was inside my head and radiated to my whole body.

India has that, it shakes you first without understanding too much, and, at the right and perfect moment comes the understanding of the experience.

It took seven years for me to understand that dream, and it was precisely when I was preparing my master's thesis in Psychopathology and Neurosciences.

I dreamed again in August 2021 of something similar. The setting was India, of course, in its Ganges, and the Taj Mahal with Goddess Durga.

The object of my thesis was consciousness, consciousness as a mental state that allows us not only to realize our existence.

I had before me, as a first challenge, to make possible the explanation about how neural activity can create a new reality totally different from the one that was had, starting from the base that consciousness is the hinge of reality.

As a lawyer, I had another challenge. Legitimize that claim. I founded it from the principle of oneness. The oneness of everything we are with everything that surrounds us.

The quantum double theory deepens the awareness that we must have of our own consciousness, since, voluntary or not, we are creators of reality. Consciousness simply is in and of itself.

Neuroscience as a new paradigm of human behavior develops the meaning of consciousness as the set of all brain processes resulting from the neural network. If there is a neural imbalance, there is a behavioral imbalance.

Consciousness has existed since the beginning of the universe and is woven by the same "universe fabric", then, when the organism dies, everything returns to its origin. It becomes an especially unifying phenomenon.

When we observe something —a person, a situation, a desire—, we turn on a small lamp there —the neuronal synapse—; the more we reinforce our attention, the more will grow the light we fix there.

This reminds me of the words Jesus said in one of his sermons to his disciples, more than 2,000 years ago: "For where your treasure is, there your heart will be also" and, therefore, that is the light we will turn on.

This is the first book in a series of three compendiums where consciousness has become the noumenon of my letters.

In this text, I present the situation of the corrupt brain as a tool for awakening to a new perspective of reality; corrupt because, in principle, it enters into a short circuit with the full development of the common good, the essential values and principles of the human being.

The corrupt lack the intelligence to know and understand their purpose in the universal design. Those who allow at least one corrupt person to exist also share the same deficiency. All the corrupt share the same impunity and, with it, the same insensitivity. For this reason, I consider the increase in corruption to be inversely proportional to the ability to be aware.

Consciousness transcends the material body. We are those lights that, when turned on, spread throughout the universe.

I pray to God that through these lines we can forge

a more comprehensive and compassionate intimacy in our evolution as individuals in society.

I leave you a little of what India left in me.

CYNTHIA CASTRO

INTRODUCTION

This work pretends to give a scientific approach, with an explanation from the neurosciences, on the corrupt brain. I affirm corruption is inherent to the human being because it depends on the neural mechanisms to which the corrupt person is accustomed. It influences the environment, how a person has been raised, and life experiences, among other factors. If the environment is corrupt, a person with similar inclinations will be more likely to commit acts of corruption without any kind of emotional asset, for example, guilt.

Decisions should be considered to be the result of feeling and thought. Therefore, an understanding of the corrupted brain can be arrived at from neurosciences. Given the little awareness of reality, and the very creation of the reality of life we have, there is also little aware-ness of the world that surrounds us because it is the one we unconsciously create. This scenario triggers a lack of responsibility in thought and in what that one feels v. gr. Those who make the same mistake are not responsible nor do they take responsibility for the consequences of their actions; therefore, they are not aware of the construction of their reality, beyond the fact we are equally responsi-ble for the unconscious.

This involves a neural mechanism stimulated, for example, by failure; when someone constantly runs the same error, then you get used to it.

The corrupt trust in their impunity, it does not matter if they are a politician, a judge, or someone from a compa-ny who is used to carrying out acts of corruption. They trust because when a subject frequently makes mistakes generates a neural mechanism in which, in one way or another, they are convinced of failure. Since there is no sanction or justice for his criminal or unethical act, the corrupt have faith he will always be like this because his neural mechanism leads him to this stimulus of impunity. Conscience inevitably derives into responsibility. So, the greater the awareness, the less corruption?

A government that tends to be corrupt is like this because its society tends to be more irresponsible since there is no sufficient sanction for reprehensible conduct.

With neurosciences, the understanding of ethics itself is approached from the neural bases, as a moral agency; this branch of science tries to find central elements of that agency, for example, the freedom of will or the substance of morality; neuroscience itself wonders about the ethical correctness of certain actions.

Ethical neuroscience talks about unraveling the cerebral bases of human behavior with the pretense of explaining it; it provides the cerebral foundation for normative ethics. Knowledge of brain mechanisms allows us to clarify scientifically what we must do morally.

To combat corruption, it is necessary to understand, first, its significance, beyond the corresponding legal and social condemnation, and it is even necessary to bear in mind that we cannot focus only on the negative aspect of the fight. On the contrary, we must recognize the objective to defend and focus on it. That way we can understand the purpose of those of us who fight corruption is not corruption itself, but the defense of Human Rights, which is what is violated by it, avoiding falling on which Friedrich Nietzsche warned and affirmed: "Whoever fights with monsters takes care not to become a monster in turn. When you look long into an abyss, it too looks into you."

Conscience, as a treasure in which we need to put our hearts and what we must exercise to create reality in defense of Human Rights, transcends human life. We adhere to that consciousness that has been explained for millennia. We hold ourselves to a consciousness that belongs to the cosmos, and the scientific explanation (from Roger Penrose —mathematical physicist— and Stuart Hameroff —anesthetist) indicates that in the cellular microtubules, we carry our consciousness attached to us. For this reason, sometimes we have that sensation or awareness of having been to certain places, or like particular cultures, even though we have never lived with them or collected memories of a life that is not this one. Thus, with this explanation, through quantum physics, Penrose and Hameroff justify life after death, with cellular microtubules, affirming consciousness survives death, transcending us. How we exercise consciousness today will be how it will resonate in the universe.

Now, corrupt: is it born or is it made? No matter

how frightening it may seem to us, how to explain and understand the lack of conscience of a corrupt person? Can neurosciences offer tools to conscience to combat corruption? Could these scientific advances promote a different social reality through a new and unified vision of humanity? If consciousness transcends death, is it possible to listen to it and activate the universal teaching that it can transmit to us?

It is, from the spirit of a new reality, that I offer, through neurosciences, a vision, a defense of Human Rights

CHAPTER I
NEUROSCIENCE

"As above, so below,
as within, so without, as the
universe, so the soul…".

Before beginning with the development of this work objective, it is important to address the concept of neuroscience in detail. What does this discipline represent in the field of human knowledge? What are its qualities and functions? Likewise, it is necessary to mention a brief history of the term, to become familiar with the content that will later be worked on around this science.

The first records regarding the studies of the human brain, or its functioning, come from Greece. Some adjudicate Hippocrates, in 400 a. C., the initial medical approach to the brain functions, since he already considered it "the basis of thought and sensations" (Romero, 2019, s. P.). However, a few other specialists give credit to Alcmeón de Crotona (cfr. Vélez, 2019, s. p.), who in the 5th-century a.C. already had an idea about the relationship between the optic nerves and their neural link with the brain.

Names such as Aristotle, Galen, Vesalius, and René Descartes, come to light in the background of the neuroscience emergence as such, since each one, from their field, made significant contributions although, in antiquity, it did not seem the analysis of that part of the human body is so relevant. Later, among all of them, the philosopher Descartes stood out, and between 1630-1650 dedicated himself to disseminating his acclaimed Mechanistic Theory on the behavior of animals.

For him, this theory would not explain the complexity of human behavior, since man, unlike animals, has an intellect and a soul given by God. That is why Descartes believed the brain controls human behavior in what is ultimately animal and that man's special capacities reside outside, in the mind ("l'esprit"). Descartes thus initiates two extraordinary lines of thought, outstanding until today. On the one hand, the mechanistic philosophy, developed by its requirements, defends that, by getting to know the machine well, the physical, including the human body and the brain, will get to know all the ins and outs of the world. On the other hand, Descartes is the father of the mind-brain problem, which is currently the subject of passionate debate among many neuroscientists. (Cavada, 2017, s. p.)

It would not be until well into the 19th century that —after the culminating era in which technological advances, added to scientific ones, in addition to discoveries and achievements in the medical field— neurology would see the light for the first time, a discipline from which it emerges as Such is the term neuroscience, which encompasses the set of sciences responsible for the study of the brain, its functions, and processes. It could be said the father of neurosciences was the Spanish doctor, Santiago Ramón y Cajal:

With the development of the microscope, and tissue fixation and staining techniques, the anatomy of the nervous system underwent a notable advance that culminated in the brilliant work of Santiago Ramón y Cajal (1852-1934). Using a silver impregnation technique developed by the Italian Camillo Golgi (1843-1926), Cajal formulated the neural doctrine—the nervous system is made up of independent cells, the neurons, which contact each other at specific locations—and built a large body of doctrine neuroanatomical. Cajal was a modern scientist, who did not limit himself to describing static structures, but rather wondered about the mechanisms that govern them. His contributions to the problems of development, degeneration, and regeneration of the nervous system are still current. The neural doctrine was confirmed from other experimental fields. (Cavada, 2017, s. p.)

The neuronal doctrine was followed by the emblematic contributions of characters such as Charles Bell and his research on phrenology, where it was indicated that each area of the brain corresponded to a set of specific functions and mental processes. It was believed the development of certain abilities corresponded to an increase in the volume of the associated brain area. In this way, he initiated a dynamic perspective of the brain, understanding the organ adapted its physical configuration to the requests of the field, reserving a larger space for the most elementary skills. As is, **it was believed intellectual and moral capacities could be recognized through the shape and size of the heads** (*cfr.* Vélez, 2019, s. p.).

François Magendie, Sir Charles Scott Sherrington, Emil Dubois-Reymond, Johannes Müller, and Hermann von Helmholtz are other key names in understanding the neuroscience field, from its first advances to its current knowledge. With each new area of the brain to which they contribute in terms of its interconnection, functions, and type of responses concerning the rest of the organs of the human body, they were completing the discipline of neurosciences.

One of the essential events for neurology's development came from the discoveries of Paul Pierre Broca (cfr. Vélez, 2019, s. p.), a French anatomist specializing in language disorders, who exposed a curious condition that, in addition, bears his last name. This was that, despite having lost her speech, his patient kept intact the ability to understand. This fact is extremely important since he established the precedent of the undeniable connection between neural functions and speech-language.

The period between the two **World Wars was translated as one of the greatest in terms of development and exponential growth in neural studies,** due to the severe disorders the use of nuclear weapons or illicit substances for torture left in the survivors. The wounded added up to miles, as did the number of consequences caused by the type of events witnessed, experienced, or executed by the protagonists, witnesses, or victims of such atrocious genocides.

According to Vélez (2019, s. p.), there were thousands of individuals with neurological consequences and, as a result, the need for neurological rehabilitation increased exponentially. This brings a new promotion for the studies in this area. In World War II, this discipline was consolidated and neuropsychological complications developed at the hands of references such as Luria. Some 20 years after the War's end, in 1962, the *Neuroscience Research Program* was launched, which was supported by an organization that brought universities from all over the world into contact. Their goal was to connect academics in the behavioral and neurological sciences.

Neurology schools or institutions received a tremendous boost in the countries most affected by the consequences of the World Wars, and greater weight began to be given to the exact location of the type of functions that were damaged, lost, or modified according to the type of injuries presented by patients.

As Cavada explained (2017, s. p.), unitary conceptions of brain function predominated in the first half of the 20th century. The most influential of this group of scholars has been Karl Lashley (1890-1958), who, in his studies of behavior in rats, appreciated that the **learning disorders caused by brain injuries depended much more on the expansion of the damage produced than on the location**

of the lesion. Lashley concluded that learning and other mental functionalities do not have a specific location in the brain and, therefore, are not likely to be associated with certain neuronal groups or cortical areas. Today, it is interpreted that Lashley's work is inadequate to study the location of functionalities, since it includes various sensory and motor processes. Damage can be compensated by other sensory functions.

In the middle of the 20th century, the emergence of the Neuroscience Society stands out, which is based in Washington and, at present, continues to be an important body in the field. Various sciences such as neuropsychology, neuroanatomy, and neurophysiology —all derived from the convergence between neurology and its various sister disciplines— have gained strength in terms of the scope of their investigations, which go deeper and deeper into the study of the understanding of the various disorders, diseases, mechanisms of operation or malfunction of mental processes.

Thus, after all the progress made since the Greeks, the Renaissance period, the World Wars, until today, **neurology, the basis of neuroscience, is defined as:**

[...] the medical specialty that studies the structure,

function, and development of the nervous system (central, peripheral, and autonomic) and muscle in a normal and pathological state, using all the clinical and instrumental techniques of study, diagnosis, and treatment currently in use or that can be developed in the future. Neurology deals comprehensively with medical care for neurological patients, teaching in all matters that affect the nervous system and research, both clinical and basic, within its field. (Sociedad Española de Neurología, 2021, s. p.)

According to Vélez (2019, s. p.), some of the most important projects related to neuroscience and its application to better understand the functioning of the human brain, its stimuli, reactions, and processes are Blue Brain (2002) from a Swiss initiative, BRAIN (2013), or The Human Brain Project (2013), financed by the European Union.

The Blue Brain project is designed for mammals, specifically whales; however, the scientists hope to contribute with their research to the progress of medical treatments applicable to people. The other two initiatives are designed to work at the human genome level. Still today, they are in experimentation and development.

Being able to explain the cerebral complexity and the

connections of the cells that are generated to each stimulus of our brain implies reaching an understanding of consciousness, because, through the computational technologies produced based on the investigations of this project, tries to discover the secrets of how the Universe perceives itself, thus materializing the universal mind.

When analyzing the brain, it was discovered that, although there is no neuron the same as another, the same way there is no brain the same as another, the latter maintains the same pattern in all human beings, capable of building a universe-like one we experience from of a series of electromagnetic frequencies, turning the brain into a universal map.

CHAPTER II
NEUROSCIENCE OF CONSCIOUSNESS

Conscience is the light of intelligence to distinguish good from evil.

CONFUCIUS

Once it is understood that neurosciences encompass much more than its base discipline - neurology - it is time to unravel the relationship between certain aspects of the human being's mind in relation to the hypothesis we are interested in testing, **how, from the approach of neurosciences, it is possible and verifiable to describe the corrupted brain,** as well as its neural reactions, in addition to its operating mechanisms.

Before thinking about how the brain of a corrupt person works, it is important to reflect on consciousness, the intangible part that inhabits, nourishes, grows, and evolves within each individual concerning the emotions they exposure to, the overcome experiences, the whole accumulation of knowledge that is stored daily, etc. So, what is consciousness?

According to Morgado (2014, s. p.), consciousness is that state of mind that allows us to understand our own life from that of other people, as well as from the facts of our context. It is nothing more than the intelligible result of the information processing that takes place inside the brain. It is something like a screen of the mind, where the brain always shows the information that we need to know at all times to direct behavior. However, this does not mean that everything the brain processes ends up producing a conscious result, since there is a lot of brain work that we will never know about. It is an intimate and personal state, since the internal state of others cannot be known; only his own. There are no scientific means that allow us to enter the consciousness of others.

To arrive at this definition, just like the history of neurology, **consciousness had to overcome obstacles since antiquity to earn its place within neuroscience** as a valuable element for understanding the mental process-es of each individual, because —as well mentioned in the definition— consciousness is as unique as the individual who possesses it. Even if the same study to thousands of people, they could all share answers or similar reactions, but with a distinctive and original component.

Neurological research on consciousness for decades has been hampered by the widespread belief that consciousness is just a special type of computer program, that is, special "software" in the "hardware" of the brain. It would just be a matter of information processing. It was a perspective, in which the study of the brain was left out. (Zumalabe, 2016, s.p.)

The neuroscience studies of consciousness pioneer, the Canadian Melvyn Goodale, who accidentally realized something else while trying to further his research on patients with visual agnosia. Natura (2021, s. p.) narrates in this regard: Goodale's initial interest was linked to the way in which the brain processes vision. However, as his work to document both visual systems that govern sight—conscious and unconscious—progressed, he drew the attention of philosophers who drew him into conversations about consciousness. Newly developed techniques for measuring brain activity allow scientists to refine their theories about what consciousness is, how it is formed in the brain, and where the parameters lie between being conscious and unconscious. And as our understanding of consciousness refines, certain scholars are beginning to develop tactics for its manipulation, with the possibility of attempting brain injuries, phobias, and psychological health conditions such as post-traumatic stress disorder (PTSD) and schizophrenia.

Consciousness research has evolved along with neuroscience, hence their relationship has become closer, since disorders linked to disabilities or problems with speech, understanding, brain injuries, and vegetative state, to name a few, have been part of the **evolutionary history between the neuroscience-consciousness nexus.**

Why is it essential to know the type of connection between neurosciences and consciousness? Due to the series of processes that unite them and help to understand the series of stimuli and reactions behind the acts of individuals; Thus, for example, it is plausible to understand the "behind the scenes" that is lived in the conscience of a corrupt before, during, and after the moment in which he commits an illegal act..

Zumalabe (2016, s. p.) explains in this regard: Initially, neurosciences were distanced from the analysis of mental phenomena. It started from the materialist principle that the mind was a product of the brain, and it was pertinent to believe that a deep understanding of the brain's functioning would provide a deep understanding of the mind. However, today these ideas have changed significantly, and the progress of neuroscience has provided new tools to approach these questions differently. Work on recording unit neuronal activity enabled by novel technologies is making it possible to describe the mind from brain performance. Behavioral and brain sciences do not eliminate humanistic values, such as freedom, nor do they leave mind and consciousness as by-products or basic epiphenomena of brain mechanisms. **Ideas are as real as neurons and have the possibility of having causal force.** Mind and consciousness maintain a position of high control over the brain processes.

It becomes important to say that the location, parts, and functions of consciousness are points of fundamental relevance to explain the reasons that lead a person to do what it does. Initially, the investigations found that consciousness does not have an immovable or fixed seat (*cfr*. Nature, 2021), although the greatest activity of consciousness has been discovered in the thalamus; if that area is injured, the person suffers a long-term, permanent, or temporary loss of consciousness, according to the severity of the damage, since those responsible for activating it are a group of cells but, above all, the perceptions stimulated by the various parts of the human body.

> Among all the conscious perceptions we have, the one that allows us to feel our own existence stands out and, with it, that our mind is something inseparable from our body since we feel it as locked in it, moving with it wherever it goes. That location of the mind in the physical limits of the body itself is a powerful perception that our brain also creates, and now we know that altering it is much easier than we might believe given its apparent solidity. (Morgado, 2014, s.p.)

There are vast analyses, articles, and works, responsible for translating how perceptions, in addition to the emotional side, unleash extremely unexpected reactions in the mind, which is why studies on sleep abound in various types of environments or with varied music. There are investigations about fear, love, anger, sadness, and depression, all from the hand of the subconscious and the unconscious, they represent them as fertile fields; day by day they become more interesting to decipher.

In this regard, here are the statements of various researchers about what mental states are:

1. "[...] Mental states, as emergent dynamic properties of brain activity, are inseparably fused with and linked to the brain activity of which they are an emergent property. Consciousness, in this view, cannot exist apart from the functioning brain" (Sperry, 1993, p. 880).

2. "It is brain processes that cause conscious experiences; a conscious state is a state the brain is in, a higher level feature of the brain itself, not a separate substance from it" (Searle, 2007, p. 15).

3. "Today, there is broad agreement that consciousness is a biological phenomenon caused by cerebral processes; what is more complicated is discerning how this causation occurs. Twenty years ago,

neuroscientists were reluctant to study the problem of consciousness, but today there are many works that rigorously address it. All of them try to discern how brain processes cause conscious states and how these states are carried out in brain structures" (Sporns, 2013; Tononi and Koch, 2008; Quian Quiroga, 2008; cited in Zumalabe, 2016, s.p.).

While it is true we are capable of experiencing multiple emotions and neural reactions, perception is one; she groups that accumulation of external, olfactory, tactile, and visual sensations. Among some of the characteristics of consciousness are the following:

- Ability to toggle between multiple thoughts at once.
- Combine fantasy with reality.
- Condition of continuity between thoughts, images, and sensations.
- Synchronization of the senses.
- Interconnection with intelligence that allows solving everyday situations or problems.
- Regulates human behavior.

- Metaconsciousness: that is, the ability to think about one's own thoughts and be aware that one has a conscience (cf. Morgado, 2014).

Conscience plays a very important role in the individual because there resides the accumulation of values inculcated, learned, or apprehended by it, a fact that, for a corrupt person, often means coming into conflict with various mental processes or contradictions. From this is also derived the failed acts, the betrayal of the unconscious, the feeling of guilt, morality, lies, as well as certain types of diseases that detonate mostly during old age.

Far away is the awareness of the entelechy in which the backward elite that represents the corrupt inhabits, saved in impunity of agreements such as "*save each other*" to maintain that system.

Today, the gauntlet of that scaffolding has been picked up by neuroscience, shedding light on the adornment of the neural mechanisms that elevate us as human beings. The above will be explained in the next section, which will address ethics and neurosciences.

CHAPTER III

NEUROSCIENCE OF ETHICS

A man without ethics is a wild beast loosed upon this world.

ALBERT CAMUSS

As has been seen, neurosciences are intrinsically connected to a diversity of related disciplines, since they are all connected in some way because the brain, its functions, and processes, affect the human being as a whole.

Starting in the 21st century, the advances made by neurosciences are not only based on internal knowledge of the brain, but also extend to understanding the consciousness of individuals through psychological medical analysis and, of course, even include the behaviors, moral judgments, as well as the set of values that govern a person's behavior, right here arises the so-called **neuroethics**.

The foundations of this science history arose as follows:

The *World Conference on Neuroethics*, sponsored by the Dana Foundation, held in San Francisco in May 2002, brought together neuroscientists, physicians, experts in neuroimaging, law and the humanities, policymakers, and media representatives. In this conference, neuroethics, understood in its double sense, as the "ethics of neuroscience" that deals with ethical, social, and legal problems associated with the development of research in neuroscience and its applications, takes on its nature. The other meaning is the "neuroscience of ethics" that aims to investigate the neural systems that are the basis of intuitions, judgments, and moral behaviors and account for conscience, self-awareness, freedom, responsibility, social mind, emotions, and empathy. (Markus, 2002; Roskies, 2002). (Garcia, 2017, 8)

For a correct differentiation of indicated areas by García, the experts chose to divide the fields of study of neuroethics according to the type of method applied or the approach, since a multiplicity of linked sciences can benefit from only one of its ramifications. It is also important to note that, currently, Biology is the discipline that houses neuroethics. Oscar (2016, p. 24) makes the following differentiation of the different areas of neuroethics:

- *Neuroethics in research.* Related to responsible conduct in neuroscience research.
- *Clinical Neuroethics.* It includes ethical challenges in the delivery of health care to neurological and psychiatric patients. Health professionals are bound by deontological codes.
- *Cultural Neuroethics.* Based on the communication and understanding of the public of neurological and psychiatric conditions.
- *Theoretical Neuroethics.* It is the theoretical and epistemological foundation of neuroethics and the impact of neuroscience research.

Despite combining all the knowledge implied by the relationship of neurosciences with ethics in the so-called neuroethics, in reality, its field of action is quite broad, hence the need to create so many subdivisions, since it continues to expand daily and with the employment of technologies has obtained a greater scope and diffusion for all the acquire advances.

Therefore, the closest definition of neuroethics is the one made by García (2017, pp. 8-9). The neuroscience of ethics can be established as basic neuroethics: **trying to understand who we are, how we think and feel, what motivates us, why we do and react in a certain way, and why we develop social and cultural constructions.** The ethics of neuroscience is applied neuroethics, it examines the repercussions, opportunities, and dangers of studies in neuroscience, neuroimaging, neuropharmacology, and brain enhancement, among others.

With the discovery of the neural processes behind the acts of an individual, a whole field of study and research possibilities opened up that has brought many answers to questions about the motives behind certain behaviors in specific subjects, doctors have benefited from this, counselors, philosophers, lawyers and all those professionals, scientists or scholars who try to reflect on violent, depressive, corrupt, abnormal behaviors or behaviors that go against the norm.

Paraphrasing Figueroa (2013, s. p.), it begins with the ethics of fast and regular life. For the average human being (das Man), moral conscience becomes the product of an objectifying internal self-doubling that achieves the figure of an audience or an authority. There is a kind of self-examination, a self-contemplation in the reaction of a spectator, who critically evaluates his behavior with an ideal, with a perfection that has its own right. Conscience scores, compares, reviews, calculates, appraises, regulates, and issues a verdict. Two elements emerge: on the one hand, a behavior of computations and expectations, like someone who runs a business and who, as a trade, is at the individual's own disposal, manages it as a private property, and has it at his fingertips without any restriction. On the other hand, it has the character of a phenomenon of conscience, of an "experience" that makes sure that it has not done anything wrong and, therefore, has no reason to feel remorse. Thus, he is convinced that there is peace of conscience, which denotes "being good" in front of himself.

Everything seems to point to the fact that, either due to genetics or our brain's biology, in particular individuals, this type of frowned upon, and even punishable behavior is more easily triggered. From this arises the importance of finding the cerebral stimuli or external elements that enhance those socially dangerous attitudes to correct, avoid, or find the best solution, which not only benefits the authorities but above all, the subject who suffers from them. Therefore, neuroethics:

> [...] tries to examine what is right or wrong, good and bad, in the treatment of the human brain, in its improvement, in the undesirable invasion of the brain, or in its worrisome manipulation. It comprises two subfields: ethical issues related to the design and conduct of neuroscientific research, and the evaluation of the ethical, legal, and social consequences derived from the studies and their practical applications. It is applied neuroethics, closely related to the ethical issues of biomedical practice, such as the research and design of clinical studies, the privacy of certain results, and the informed consent of the patient to participate in the research. In the conference papers publication, five thematic fields were identified: the problem of self-awareness and personal identity, the social and legal implications, research and applications in areas such as pharma-

cology and clinics, the public reception of these issues, and the future of the new discipline. (García, 2017, 9)

It is worth mentioning that, at all times, the treatment of the information handled by neuroethics is confidential, because far from seeking social disintegration or, in any case, labeling people for the type of corrupt behavior, depressive or otherwise, its purpose is conciliation, help to a **better understanding of each individual's self in order to establish support, control or improvement mechanisms for these behaviors.**

The neurosciences linked to ethics are also concerned with deciphering the social codes that for thousands of years have been instilled from generation to generation and have been recorded in the minds of individuals — in most cases for the worse—, since the racial question, for example, which has tried to be completely eradicated for the benefit of the classist disappearance of humans, some people still present an unconscious reaction of fear, anger, anger or rejection when, without knowing another person; solely by its color, these sensations are evoked.

During embryological development, our moral capacities are prepared, but they are not fully configured at birth. These capacities are regulated in the social and cultural world we live in until reaching adulthood. It is the result of the organism's interaction with its physical and social environment. (Oscar, 2016, 28)

Precisely because the individual is born in a "pure" state and becomes what his experience in the world and within society makes him, it is that, within neuroethics, there are also limits to what is considered correct to apply, know or treat and the opposite side, since whenever there is a possibility of damage, **neuroethics has established mechanisms to stop or minimize the damage to the individual,** their environment, the specialists, and the authorities involved.

García (2017, p. 11) reflects that another problem of the ethics of neuroscience is related to brain improvement through genetics, brain training, or psychotropic drugs. There is an overriding question: Should parents be allowed to engineer their children through genetic engineering? The training and improvement of bodily skills or mental abilities can be achieved through effort and practice, with or without artificial brain enhancement procedures. However, interventions through drugs to be able to perform or design better physical abilities are questioned, as shown by anti-doping controls in competitions. The improvement of the brain through drugs exposes serious drawbacks; the use of drugs or other neuroscientific techniques implies concern about stability and unwanted sequels. In addition, there is concern about the social impacts brain optimization could produce, harming our way of life, as well as values and behavior patterns.

At present, issues such as abortion, euthanasia, genetic improvement, altering DNA, perfecting or enhancing certain characteristics in human beings, postponing aging, and trying to prolong life, among others, continue to be the subject of heated debates. Even today, it is taboo to raise your voice on issues such as those mentioned above, even in disciplines as current as those covered by neurosciences.

Considering the above, neuroethics still has a lot of work to do. Regarding the work's objective, the explanation about the corrupt brain, it would be pertinent to mention it is the neuroscience part of ethics that is responsible for dealing with this issue since its main task is precisely to inquire about the neurological bases and the behavior, moral or value judgments surrounding an individual's acts; without this implying justifying and circumscribing corruption to biological issues of character deviation or a defective basic education. It is by recognizing the social environment where ethical deviations are encouraged, and understanding the neurobiological bases of the individual that evidences a deterioration in the capacity for moral judgment with which each person, exercising their free will, decides to be corrupt.

After this brief introduction to the disciplines that will be used to develop the subject, it will delve into the brain of a corrupt individual.

CHAPTER IV
CORRUPTION

Corruption is the sole
cause of all crises.

Until now, each of the disciplines that will intervene in the development of the functioning of a corrupt brain and, above all, the role that neuroscience plays in it, have been explained separately. To start with this section, it is important to understand **what corruption is**. According to the newspaper *El País* (2016), corruption defined from a social sphere refers to: "a shared, expanded and tolerated belief that the use of the public function is for the benefit of oneself, of one's family and friends" (s.p.).

This behavior linked to neurological stimuli is not exclusive to the human species. Investigations have determined that some species in nature also share the same symptoms; for example, bees, some kinds of chimpanzees, and ants (*cfr.* Fernández, 2020).

The human brain capacity limits have not yet been fully investigated. In this sense, **corruption is precisely the result of the evolution - albeit negative - of the behavior of an individual in relation to the rest of the members of his society.** According to Ramirez *et al.* (2014, s. p.):

Corruption is the action of damaging, deteriorating, sickening, perverting, depraving, spoiling, and manipulating someone for unhealthy purposes, altering and disrupting their identity, consciously or unconsciously favoring their complicity. **This action eliminates the creative values in a legitimate, authentic ethic, of one, of the other, of the environment, and of society.** Despite the fact that popularity and temporary material goods were obtained through corrupt acts, those corrupt individuals are beings with personality disorders who enter into a psychiatric conflict for an affective and emotional reason, having taken advantage of people for their benefit. [*added emphasis*].

The process that takes place inside the brain of a corrupt individual shows that said act is not natural at first, since no human being likes to experience negative or unpleasant sensations, but with time and the frequency with which the pattern is repeated, the brain ends up getting used to stopping the inhibitory mechanisms that produce stimuli of discomfort, guilt, remorse, displeasure:

The cerebral amygdala has always been related to emotions and is part of the limbic system, which is a set of nuclei in the brain responsible for affection, memory, the instinct of conservation, and the reactions of other parts of the organism and the relationship with the environment, at the time of performing an action. Based on these functions of the amygdala, **the researchers concluded that activity in this brain structure is directly related to dishonesty**. [*added emphasis*]. (Fernández, 2020, s. p.)

The corruption process is directly linked to all the neurotransmitters that control emotional stimuli. In addition, the speed at which the accumulation of sensations related to an act of corruption is generated is superior to any thought or rational operation executed, since the adrenaline that is mixed with the knowledge or awareness of knowing the type of fact that is being carried out, triggers greater effectiveness in terms of the reactions of the subjects involved. Bertone (2018, s. p.) lo explains it as follows:

In addition to the above, and contrary to what might be believed, corrupt people usually have quite high levels of empathy compared to those of an average subject, since they are more susceptible to the misfortunes or problems of social minorities, hence the politicians, religious authorities or executives of international or transnational companies are among the best examples.

> However, usually, **the type of individuals who tend to corruption suffer from narcissism or bipolar disorders, since their personality is of the controlling type**. They are skilled emotional manipulators and "charming" treatment: "In what they have shown significant deficiencies is on being able to feel what they cause in the other, this allows them, for example, to collect bribes in a work, even knowing this can affect the development and/or well-being of a vulnerable population without feeling remorse." (Bertone, 2018, s. p.).

The foregoing is also linked to the type of education, personal experiences, as well as the set of values inherent in their way of being, although in the case of the corrupt, their childhood background is usually characterized by a marked lack of values or stimuli sufficiently reinforced to leave a positive imprint at the neural level bigger than the impulses to stop the act of committing a crime.

> Corruption is a condition since, although it is an individual decision to commit acts of this type, in reality, it is not just a singular deviant conduct. In other words, there are no corrupt human beings, but a corrupt society in which human beings (disposed to corruption) act. In a study conducted by researcher Dan Ariely, it was shown that a small bribe can have a dramatic influence on an individual's moral behavior. [*added emphasis*]. (*El País*, 2016, s. p.)

Added to the set of traits that have been discussed, **a corrupt is distinguished by the following characteristics:**

- Norms and social agreements are not respected.
- They adapt or deviate from social or moral codes for the convenience or benefit of those close to them.

- They choose to commit illegal acts in a hidden, stealthy manner, with great secrecy in the public eye.
- Their reactions, when observed, can trigger extreme insecurity, exacerbated anger, or self-consciousness.
- Their emotional state or way of life is directly connected to the level of corrupt acts they are capable of performing.
- Everyone begins to commit crimes, usually thanks to bribes, small infractions, or "bites" until they reach major crimes such as money laundering, extortion, fraud, etc.
- They come from family contexts with deprivations, emotional gaps, or inappropriate or socially frowned upon codes of behavior that were never corrected or sanctioned.
- They tend to make corruption a normal way of life.
- They display predatory, abusive, and intolerant behaviors.
- They have a tendency (easiness) to infect or influence the most intimate and trusted members of their entourage towards corruption. (see La Información, 2016; Moscote, 2018).

Almost entirely, **it is thanks to neuroscience that it has been possible to investigate, not only the type of traits that differentiate the corrupt from other individuals, but also the processes developed from within them,** because also through Neurosciences have managed to determine the affected regions or the places where corruption is housed.

> The issue of corruption has been studied from sociology and political science, from history and law. But it is important to take into account that human behavior can have biological, psychological, cultural, and social causes at the same time, which interact to influence and are not disjunctive. (*El País*, 2016, s. p.)

In order to reveal signs of potentially corrupt behavior, the studies indicate a series of experiments carried out with groups of sample subjects, where certain types of acts susceptible to corruption are put into practice, and through controlled statistics, they are subjected to provocations to commit illicit acts against the other participants, knowing they will receive for each act executed, a certain monetary retribution that increases according to the aptitudes presented at the individual level.

> In 2014, the scientific journal *Frontiers in Behavioral Neuroscience* published the result of an experiment in which skin conductance, a measure of general emotional variation, was computed when offering, receiving, or waiting to see if a bribe discovered the fact of corruption in which someone was involved. An auction was simulated and people were given the ability to bribe the auctioneer to make a profit. The first few times, they could bribe freely, but then the loser could demand to inspect the operation. Among the results, it was found that both auction-eers and bribers were less corrupt when they knew they could be observed. In addition, electrodermal activity increased when the person made a positive, honest, and prosocial decision. The gaze of the other (or the possible gaze of the other) is what sanctions opportunism. (*El País*, 2016, s. p.)

As the quote explains, **the key element, and where the cure or at least an alternative solution to corrupt** behavior probably resides, is in public scrutiny, the gaze, recognition, or social exposure, since it implies a highly relevant term speaking of a neurological degree: the sanction.

> If there is no social sanction, the mechanism of rewards and punishments is lost, and the crime is naturalized. Through the study of our evolutionary behavior and the resolution of moral dilemmas, it was observed that, regardless of culture, age, social class, or religion, man is corrupt by nature: he thinks first of his own good and then considers moral and social rules, his punishments and perceptions of him. Not carrying out acts of corruption implies a prosocial attitude, as opposed to an attitude exclusively in pursuit of the individual good. The law and the social perspective positively influence our conduct. (Fernández, 2020, s. p.)

It is true that **corruption, in addition to being a behavior or a way of life, can also be considered a defensive social response to pressure, lack, and emotional emptiness,** since mainly, the interaction with the environment, the hierarchical environment that leads to each subject to live with thousands of daily stimuli of a positive or negative nature or bombardments from the mass media, determines many of the guidelines that lead or push subjects to lean towards illegal practices before following the path marked as the ideal or the less accepted by the majority:

> Corruption seems to take power within the political territory for most people, however, it is found in excess of actions within the environment, not only in the political sphere but also in the social sphere, regarding health, within an economic profile, administratively and painfully, in the family circle. There must be something in the mind of the corrupt that makes him insensitive to the act of corruption and its consequences, there must be something else in the neurobiology of the corrupt that justifies his rotten actions. If honesty is among the noblest of virtues, then corruption is among the most regrettable behaviors of human beings. We did not realize corruption was not an unexpected threat or a surprise scourge, but that it had been our inveter-

ate and sordid way from the beginning. (Ramírez, 2014, s. p.)

It is also fair to recognize that corruption is born within society and, therefore, the studies that address the "cure" of this evil are focused on the series of factors that, in short, can reverse this type of bad behavior pattern that increase with the status of the nation where they are committed more often, in addition to the various sectors such as economic, commercial, labor, etc.

The role played by the neurosciences in terms of understanding the processes through which a corrupt being goes through, has been essential to put into practice stimuli and mechanisms that reverse or measure the scope of this illegal behavior to establish controls, in addition to keeping the subjects probably to develop it, although the truth is that it is a titanic task, since up to now, it is known that all living beings are prone to carry out certain types of corrupt acts at some time in their lives. This is how Moscote questions (2018, s. p.):

Finally, the big question is: can a corrupt person be rehabilitated? Hardly in a society like ours, where some social sectors look favorably on those who make money easily, on the clever person who can get millions with minimal effort, regardless of the pain and suffering that he is inflicting on his compatriots who are harmed when money for health, education, water, and social investment disappears. From neurosciences, there are many challenges to understanding this kind of behavior that in itself indicates our politicians are sick people at the brain level. We require continuous effort to show our children that the path of decent work is the key to a hopeful tomorrow.

Although the forecasts certainly indicate negative results for others, it is true that if corruption is seen as a disease, in principle we would detract from the decision made by a corrupt person regarding the acts they commit and, **the challenge of neurosciences and sister disciplines** such as ethics, psychology, biology, human sciences, sociology, **would reside precisely in proposing cures, treatments, strategies to provide subjects with this condition with alternatives that return them to the right path, or at least emphatically warn them of** the possibility of being penalized or receiving harsher sentences in line with the acts they have carried out or plan to carry out.

Immanuel Kant, a Prussian philosopher and scientist, indicates in his in-depth analysis of morality that corruption can be faced with the publicity of public acts and their transparency. He indicates corruption is in sync with the immorality of the political moralist, who considers morality to be only demagogic and rhetorical.

Corruption, latent in the public and private spheres, although with different acts, converge in the intention of obtaining benefits that without these illegal acts would be impossible to achieve.

Next, we will delve deeper into the link between the various neuroscience theories and corruption, all with the aim of verifying the premise of this research that neuroscience is the ideal discipline to understand the corrupt brain, as well as explain everything that happens during the initiation, development, and establishment of this conduct in the corrupt.

CHAPTER V
RELATIONSHIP BETWEEN NEUROSCIENCE AND CORRUPTION

If corruption is a disease,
then transparency is a central
part of its treatment

KOFI ANNAN

In the previous chapter, a brief analysis of corruption was addressed, including the way in which it is defined, the characteristics that distinguish the subjects exposed to carrying it out, as well as a brief preamble regarding the processes that are deployed at the neurological level. Now it is the turn to deepen regarding its link with neurosciences.

Societies, through their specialists and the media, make efforts to explain such events by appealing to ethical, and often social and political issues. It is, however, much more complicated than it seems. **Is corruption an inherent characteristic of the human condition? Or is it something socia-**

lly constructed thanks to the environment that surrounds us? What happens in our brain and body when we perpetrate a corrupt act? At what point do we go from good to bad? What the different disciplines say, not only humanists, can open our eyes and understand these acts in a closer way, and less attributable only to the ruling classes [added emphasis]. (Meza, 2018, s. p.)

However, before delving into the relationship between neuroscience and corruption, it is essential to **know the neurofunctional model of consciousness, as well as its neurophysiological and cognitive bases.**[1]

Why is it important to define and characterize the neurofunctional model of consciousness? First, the focus on the link between consciousness and neural activity has been warned in recent years, which modifies the perspective we can have on the matter. Second, to better understand the processes that occur in the brain in the formation of consciousness.

---

1   U. León-Domínguez y J. León-Carrión (2019). The concepts that are discussed below are derived from this article.

Experiments carried out in animals, as well as in patients with brain damage from functional neuro-imaging, show the brain structures and networks that makeup consciousness. However, despite experiments and neuroimaging, no theory adequately understands consciousness; therefore, U. León-Domínguez and J. León-Carrión (2019) offer a theoretical framework that can constitute the empirical knowledge of consciousness in a neurofunctional model of it, which represents it as an epiphenomenon resulting from the activation of various neural loops made up of specific brain structures and networks fed by their own operations:

> The ascending activating reticular system, the thal-amocortical networks, and the cortico-cortical networks support differentiated cognitive process-es, although highly dependent and basic to the final experience of consciousness. All these systems form a single physiological space where the individual can deploy different cognitive abilities that allow the emergence of complex behaviors such as language, thought, and social cognition. (León-Domínguez and León-Carrión, 2019, s. p.)

According to these neuroscientists, how can we define consciousness? "Consciousness is a physiological state of the nervous system that varies according to the temporal and spatial domain of its neural operations, finally allowing the appearance of complex and conscious behaviors" (León-Domínguez and León-Carrión, 2019). Complex behaviors can be covered —thoughts— and not covered —motor behaviors—.

Consciousness has two qualities:

- The alert level, also known as *arousal*. It is the level of energy/body activation/psychological activation at a given moment. The absence of alert implies the absence of consciousness, v. gr. when sleeping or when we are anesthetized. Physiological activation is a requirement to process information correctly.
- The experience of consciousness —*awareness*— is the human being's ability to perceive both internal and external states (environment) and, furthermore, intervene in them.

These two qualities depend on the functional state

of the brain networks (León-Domínguez and León-Carrión, 2019).

The **thalamus** is the primordial element of the thalamocortical system. Why? Because it functions as a **regulator of brain activity** and participates —directly and indirectly— in brain operations. **It is made up of three nuclear groups** (León-Domínguez and León-Carrión, 2019):

- **First order or relay group:** they make connections to certain sensory and motor regions of the cortex.
- **Higher order or associative group:** they receive and project efferent and afferent connections to the cortex.
- **Non-specific groups:** They have connections throughout the brain, which regulate specific cognitive functions that are a fundamental part of understanding consciousness.

The main non-specific nuclei of the thalamus are:

- **The Thalamic Reticular Nucleus (NRT):** it is the main regulatory nucleus of the thalamus for attentional processes. It is divided into the sensory region and the motor region. The first modulates attention from connections with the prefrontal cortex; the second is related to limbic and motor processes:

> Different authors suggest that the function of NRT in attentional processes is to act as an 'attentional focus' or 'attentional gate' due to its ability to regulate the sensory information that reaches consciousness. [...] The NRT is a basic structure in selective attention due to its ability to block attentional processes of the up-down and bottom-up type through the inhibition of different thalamic nuclei that are involved in the formation of the contents of consciousness [...]. Short-term synaptic plasticity in NRT neurons is involved in the formation of temporary connections between several brain areas that construct the primary conscious content of attention. (León-Domínguez and León-Carrión, 2019, s. p.)

• **The Intralaminar Nuclei (ILN):** are associated with the modulation of cortical activity and the restoration of consciousness. Its anterior region is related to motor tasks and the posterior region organizes limbic, motor, and associative information. It also has relevance in the integration of affective functions. Various experiments have stimulated these nuclei to try to restore the consciousness of patients with related problems; however, only a behavioral improvement was observed, but without awareness; In short, these nuclei regulate alertness and motor programming, but by themselves, they do not generate consciousness.

- **The Midline Nuclei of the Thalamus (NMT):** are linked to memory and emotional processes. They contribute to learning, memory consolidation, and cognitive flexibility. These nuclei can mediate in the selection of appropriate behavior in accordance with external stimuli:

The conscious perception of a consciousness content does not occur spontaneously but is the result of a hierarchical and cumulative activation that begins in the posterior cerebral regions and spreads to the anterior cortical regions depending on certain physiological characteristics in the reverberation of certain cortico-cortical networks. (León-Domínguez and León-Carrión, 2019, s. p.)

For the conscious processing of the consciousness contents, cortico-cortical networks are involved. **When the content of consciousness is formed by the hindbrain, it is consciously maintained and manipulated by cortico-cortical networks, primarily through the *Default Neural Network (RND)*.** This network has traditionally been related to self-referenced thoughts or thoughts that do not require information from the outside. However, current studies show that the RND does process extrinsic information, since it is involved in certain attentional processes and in the evocation of memories, this is because it integrates spatial, self-referenced, and temporal information. In this way, it has a fundamental role in all the cognitive processes of the brain, regardless of the level of processing (León-Domínguez and León-Carrión, 2019):

> Among all the cortico-cortical networks, the ones with the greatest physiological weight in complex information processing are the frontoparietal central executive network, the dorsal attentional network, and the relevance assignment network. All these networks, including the RND, share overlapping

regions that allow the transfer of physiological resources from one network to another, depending on the quality of the ongoing cognitive activity. **The result of the continuous interaction between all these networks (especially between the RND and the central executive network) will ultimately define the individual's experience of consciousness** [added emphasis]. (León-Domínguez and León-Carrión, 2019, s. p.)

In a related study, a patient in a vegetative state improved the minimally conscious state by increasing connectivity between the hindbrain and forebrain. This indicates the relationship of the hindbrain with the forebrain in long-distance neural networks is fundamental for a stable and continuous consciousness (León-Domínguez and León-Carrión, 2019).

In the last third of the 20th century and the 21st century, various theories of consciousness have been developed. They agree that consciousness arises from brain activity, it is a global process of the brain, and it is linked to higher cognitive functions. León-Domínguez and León-Carrión (2019) propose a neurofunctional model of consciousness based on the theories developed, for which they start from the idea that the lower and upper structures of the brain forms neural loops that feed back their operations to adjust the neural activation and regulate behavior. In this way, consciousness is linked to a closed-loop neural network rather than an emergent producer of sensory input.

The authors said they represent the neurofunctional model of consciousness as follows:

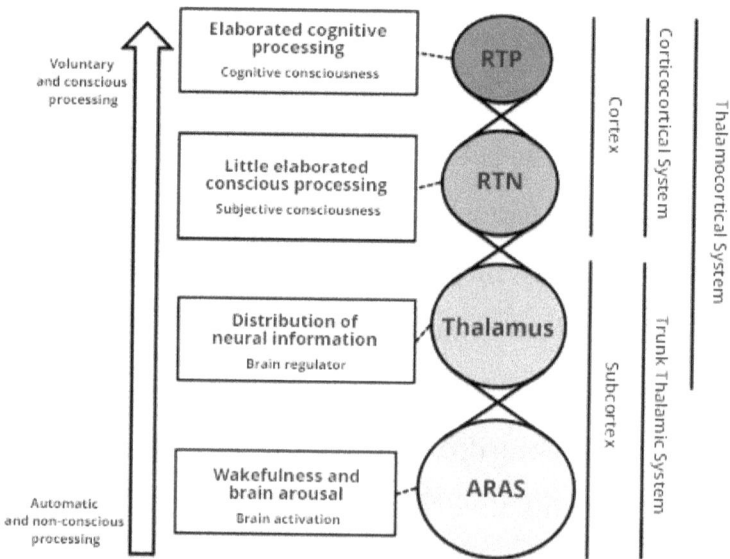

Figure 1. Neurofunctional model of consciousness (León-Domínguez and León-Carrión, 2019, s. p.).

According to León-Domínguez and León-Carrión (2019), the model shows the following characteristics: consciousness is a phenomenological quality that arises from the sequential activation of different brain networks, which function as loops —or neural cycles— that 'report' their operations to higher and lower levels. In the model, the lower loop is the ascending reticular activator system (ARAS); its projections to the thalamus and hypothalamus structure the trunk-thalamic system, which enables and allows brain activity.

The thalamus regulates the flow of neural information arriving via different pathways from the brain stem, which it integrates with cortical inputs and projects them back to the cerebral cortex. These structure the thalamocortical system, which is responsible for mediating the flow of neural information throughout the brain. The **cortex** is made up of the cortico-cortical system, which is composed of **negative task networks** (RTN) and **positive task networks** (RTP). The first are those that dominate cortical activity in resting states, where there is low processing of information from the outside. Once the external demand predominates in the general processing of brain activity, positive task networks are activated, which allow more complex and elaborate processing of information. These networks shape different contents of consciousness into plans and verbal reports by regulating higher cognitive processes. (León-Domínguez y León-Carrión, 2019).

The model is made up of four loops (León-Domínguez and León-Carrión, 2019):

- The **first** neuronal loop of the neurofunctional model is constituted by the ascending reticular activator system and its connections with the non-specific nuclei of the thalamus and hypothalamus.
- The **second** loop would be formed by the thalamus, integrated, in turn, by the non-specific nuclei of the thalamus and the bidirectional connections that perpetuate the cerebral cortex and subcortex.
- The **third** loop is made up of negative task networks, which dominate global cortical activity in rest states and with low cognitive load, such as self-referenced thoughts. The main negative task network is the RND, which is a possible neurophysiological marker of consciousness.
- The **fourth** neural loop would be made up of posi-

tive task networks, which are activated when neural processing needs increase due to greater cognitive demand. At times like this, positive task networks dominate cortical activity to the detriment of negative task networks. This increase occurs when the subject has to process information from the outside to carry out conscious and purposeful plans.

Cognitive functions cannot suspect consciousness by themselves; on the contrary, they are a consequence. When the content of consciousness is ready to be manipulated, we have a phase known as "cognitive consciousness", which is far from subjective awareness or conscious perception of the contents. Therefore, the role played by the prefrontal cortex is essential: first, it controls and organizes conscious information into complete behaviors; second, the degree of connectivity with the hindbrain will determine the individual's experience of consciousness (León-Domínguez and León-Carrión, 2019).

Summarizing, in the authors' words, the neurofunctional model is explained as follows:

The neurofunctional model of consciousness is a theoretical proposal that offers a framework from which to approach consciousness from a neuro-physiological perspective based on the interaction of the main brain structures and networks. **This model understands consciousness as a sequence of neural events** that increase in complexity as the processing of sensory information progresses from lower to higher brain structures. **These structures are integrated into large brain networks forming neural loops** that feed back among themselves, updating their functional states depending on the results of their own neural operations. As a result, **we obtain a model divided into loops or neural cycles, where each one contributes a layer of procedural complexity** that gives sensory information a new phenomenological dimension until it is integrated into a single content of consciousness, ready to be incorporated by higher cognitive functions in thoughts or complex motor plans. **This model can be useful for professionals who require a theoretical framework on which to base their clinical evaluations or experimental designs, or even as**

a teaching guide for university subjects [added emphasis]. (León-Domínguez and León-Carrión, 2019, s. p.)

Related to the topic of this chapter, **corruption is not found innately in human beings; it is a conduct, a behavior, that is apprehended through the bad example of the members who practice it, whether in the family, work or friendly environment**. It can be developed by influence, direct observation, blackmail, self-will in the face of some pressure, lack or simply by imitation and a desire to obtain goods, money or better positions without so much effort: "Corruption finds its breeding ground in two main components: the scruple's absence on the corrupt and impunity, motivated is in a lax legislation or in the occasional collusion with the powers that should penalize it" (Orellana, 2018, s. p.).

Then, **the real cause of corruption is an external stimulus on the social environment side, in which the subjects operate on a daily basis** and that gradually increases as the seriousness of the crimes grows in terms of their implementation and, above all, when they are successful and go unpunished, because precisely, the biggest problem in the face of this condition lies in the null case by the authorities: there is no follow-up, strict regulations or lasting and impartial sanctions for the culprits.

From the neuroscience approach, there is a whole body of research that has shed light on the brain functioning of a corrupt person, from its first steps to when the frequency of this type of practice has already turned them into professionals lacking in shame or dissimulation. **What sections of the brain are involved in this fact? First, is the cerebral amygdala.**

> The amygdala is a region of the brain in charge of human emotions. It is part of the limbic system, which is made up of a set of nodes or nuclei in charge of affective life, the instinct to have, the development of memory, and the link that connects the environment with the organs before executing any action. It also has under his guardianship the instinctive control of emphatically accepting or rejecting the lived experiences (*cfr.* Huerta, 2016, s. p.).

The most relevant thing about this brain region is here resides the mechanism that generates the sensations of fear, uncertainty, or restlessness when the individual is faced with an illegal, immoral, or censored situation by the public gaze:

> This means that if a person crosses the admissible ethical-moral line, and commits an action for which he obtains a high personal benefit and all this does not generate any harmful results, there will be no record of threat or alarm in his brain, so the violation committed will no longer be considered dangerous by the amygdala. (Orellana, 2018, s. p.)

At cerebral level stimuli, with the constancy of corruption, the natural breaks the amygdala emits gradually disappear out of habit; then, the nervous system relaxes, as well as the self-perception about considering these acts bad or reprehensible. Psychologically, a series of reactions will also be triggered, and the discomfort experienced at the beginning is replaced by the adrenaline of knowing that the crime will be carried out successfully: "In short, in those individuals whose behavior is not in line with their ethical principles, a mechanism will be triggered consisting in which the repetition of any type of transgression relaxes and dissipates their moral code, reduces the sensitivity of the amygdala and turns the infraction into a daily norm" (Orellana, 2018, s. p.).

An important fact in this regard is that, although all living beings have the predisposition to become corrupt, **this tendency is not something you are born with or that results very severely**. The brain has fixed patterns on which tools, techniques, or survival strategies are created in the face of daily experiences to which the individual will be exposed. However, these can be changed or adapted, this is called: "brain plasticity".

> The difference in the answers in moral aspects within a society depends on the neural circuits' sensitivity, which as a unit is called personality and that is nothing more than the sum of the inherited temperament and the character molded by the culture [...]; in other words, the ethical aspects depend on the specific conditions of the individual and the environment in which they operate. It has also been proven that abuse, stress, and family detachment in early child-

hood prevent the formation of circuits that determine the perceptual and emotional, on which the anticipatory emotional system is built, which is the biological basis of ethics and the bottom line abuse, ambiguous authority, punishment, lack of positive reinforcement in childhood, and dysfunctional family life impede the development of skills for socializing, decision-making, and coping [added emphasis]. (Fernández, 2020, s. p.)

It is due to the failure in the early stages of the infant's life that, as he grows up, reflects an emptiness in his internal constitution, which makes him fragile before the outside world, with antisocial cultural patterns and, therefore, **moving towards corruption is not a real difficulty**. Hence, the subsequent response of this class of individuals is that of total detachment, disinterest, indifference, manipulation, abuse, or maltreatment toward their peers.

Neurologists explain that, in the same way in which corruption occurs, **correction processes must be oriented to return the subject to the right path through quality education and full childhood, in addition to**

promoting a good growth environment, both family, friendship, and work.

When a corrupt is exposed, the kind of reactions are usually variants; They typically display the following kinds of behaviors:

- There is no real awareness of the transgressive act.
- Justifies the action on the grounds that there was a good reason for doing it.
- Always think there is the possibility of returning to the right path, believing he has a permanent escape valve.
- Presents himself to others as a winner, when he is actually a manipulative liar.
- Permanently presents a double face and appearance; he strives to build an image of social health through his achievements obtained through corrupt acts, of which no one has found out (see Orellana, 2018).

According to certain studies carried out by communities of neurologists, **there is a clear response at the level of the epidermis that reveals a corrupt being. This is due to the degree of conductivity produced during**

the experimentation of extreme physiological states and reveals that, without the procedure of the public sanction granted by public gaze or scrutiny, the corrupt are in an ideal state to carry out their crimes without any setbacks. It is worth mentioning that, when it comes to levels, political leaders take the top positions:

> It is also interesting to note the psychiatric approach given to corruption and other degeneration in the power of political leaders by the British neuroscientist, physician, and politician David Owen. For the latter, the corruption of a political leader with the power of authority comes within the framework of a picture that he calls Hubris Syndrome and that he developed in an article in Brain magazine in 2009 and his book *The Hubris Syndrome: Bush, Blair and the intoxication of power.* **Excessive pride and arrogance could lead the politician to border on mental instability,** according to Owen [added emphasis]. (Meza, 2018, s.p.)

Given this context provided by the joint work of the neurosciences, it is clear that corruption is not in itself the core of the problem, since there are many specialists who question **why corruption occurs disproportionately in certain societies, and not even in others it doesn't even exist, or the crime rates are low**. Opposite poles of the same coin with a quite sensible answer: **corruption is born, grows, and feeds within those societies that lack solid norms, values, and principles that respect both individuals and the authorities and institutions that represent them.**

The levels of tolerance for this type of practice are the same that define the degree of corruption social systems allow among their citizens:

> Qualitative interviews carried out with experts in corruption and different areas (politics, foreign trade, pharmaceutical, construction industry, and sports), can show a common trend of corrupt organizations. This was done by two psychologists, and they concluded that **corrupt organizations often perceive themselves as being in the middle of a war, which makes them maintain the attitude that the end justifies the means.** This has implications for the overall values of the organization:

rationalize unethical behavior and punish those who are not corrupt [added emphasis]. (El País, 2016, s.p.)

Facts such as those mentioned by *El País* are the ones that will eventually **turn the most corrupt societies against their honest or just members,** since they will **adopt a series of attitudes such as those described below:**

- Honest individuals are often mocked and humiliated by the corrupt at all levels.
- They admire corrupt behaviors because they brazenly disguise the ease with which they obtain the means or the monetary resource, evading authority without suffering consequences for it.
- They generate fear of free expression, as they tend to apply reprisals.
- They sow insecurity among honest members regarding the correct practices or way of life.
- They punish or censor anyone who does not allow themselves to be influenced by these bad behaviors or does not accept bribes or extortion.

- His shield is diplomatic immunity or jurisdiction.
- They persecute the honest until they corrupt or disappear.
- Frequently, due to the level of care received, they ended up being more registered than model citizens (see Meza, 2018).

After reviewing the postulates corruption implies in an individual at all levels, **it is possible to conclude this section by highlighting the enormous support the intervention of neurosciences has represented when translating the set of brain sections involved with this evil,** as well as make available to specialists the type of stimuli that promote corruption as a warning that contributes in terms of the formation of techniques to combat, stop or disappear this social disease that every day is responsible for putting entire societies in check massively without nobody really cares about participating in the fight to eradicate the illegal practices that it entails.

Christoph Stefes, a professor of political science at the University of Colorado, says history teaches that one way to fight systemic corruption is to create "islands of honesty" in society, led by honest individuals, surrounded by honest people, and able to mobilize large honest segments of the population, tipping the balance of society to the side of honesty. (Huerta, 2016, s.p.)

Despite the greater pressure that exists in society, it is important to unite individuals, their institutions and the sciences at the service of motivated research to generate greater well-being in the population in order to join efforts and instill in the younger generations an education sufficiently solid, loaded with values to be able to fight head-on against this evil and not give in to its reprehensible practices disguised as false heroism or promises of a better life.

In addition to contributing an effort with young people, neurosciences are advancing more and more, predicting better and more effective results that will contribute to treatments to be able to return subjects in adulthood to the right path, where lives are not sacrificed to give comforts or privileges to a reduction focused on increasing or corroding the foundations of societies today. The internal reflection of each one is necessary to be able to strengthen the willpower and all that is good without falling into the path of what is easy, from which it is difficult to return without getting hurt, or alive in extreme cases.

CHAPTER VI

CONSCIOUSNESS

Conscience makes us betray, accuse,
and fight against ourselves, and for want
of other witnesses, to give evidence against
ourselves.

MICHEL DE MONTAIGNE

In the second chapter of this research work, some aspects related to consciousness were addressed; for example, its definition, emergence, the type of obstacles it faced in its beginnings, studies, characteristics, names of pioneers in the field, background, its famous and controversial location, the type of emotions, reactions and stimuli it undergoes when it comes to the execution of illegal acts due to the set of mechanisms, in addition to processes triggered by these.

Well then, consciousness is a mental state that resides, born, develops, grows, and dies in every human being. It is capable of carrying out multiple tasks simultaneously, as well as dealing with the control and storage of values or the "moral" part of the individual.

It specializes in helping the subject to be aware of himself, his peers and the sociocultural environment in which he develops: "It is something like a mental screen where the brain continuously presents the information that we need to know at all times to guide behavior"(Morgado, 2014, s.p.).

Consciousness has great qualities, but also limits; one of them is that it is unique and unrepeatable, since there are no two alike for every person on the planet. This applies in the same way to the totality of what it represents; that is, you can only learn your own, not that of others.

From the foregoing, the studies on restlessness in relation to individuals, mental illnesses or conditions related to disorders of the brain or psyche and their real conscious capacity, also mentioned in the second section of this document, can be deduced.

As Morgado (2014) rightly points out: "One of the most special characteristics of human consciousness is being aware of itself, that is, we are not only aware, but that we are also aware that we are aware and can think about our own thoughts" (s. p.).

Precisely because of this type of quality is that the

conscience of the human being becomes so complex when it comes to infringing the pre-established behaviors, to call them in some way, because at brain level the most unexpected reactions are triggered, detonated by the adrenaline, at the moment we know that we are in danger or at risk of being exposed or surprised in the crime.

Investigations indicate the lack of a specific type of conscience that allows separating the senses to experience the accumulation of stimuli or perceptions in parts when corruption has contaminated an individual, hence it is said that emotions feel stronger when they are prohibited things, taboos or illegal acts: "In reality, being conscious places us before what Chalmers has called the 'soft problem' and the 'hard problem' of consciousness. The first refers to aspects such as wakefulness, attention or knowledge, and the second to concepts as complex as self-awareness, 'neural self' or social cognition" (Tirapu, 2016, s. p.).

In the end, it is worth remembering that conscience ends up adapting to the subject if corrupt acts are carried out frequently or regularly and, instead of feeling in danger or threatened, it endows the subject with courage, security, excessive confidence or arrogance in order to protect it and transform it into a skilled being, capable of coming out ahead of corruption and all related situations, or at least most, that may arise.

The second section of this paper mentions most specialists have associated the location of consciousness with the thalamus, given the kind of perceptions displayed, the type of impulses experienced by consciousness or the multiple sensations that a varied sample of studied test subjects goes through; however,

> A team of researchers from the University of Surrey, led by Professor Johnjoe McFadden, published the new theory in the journal Neuroscience of Consciousness. There, the specialists stated that consciousness is not found in the brain but in the electromagnetic energy generated by electrical impulses shared between neurons. The study suggests that human consciousness, the most complex product of the body's nervous activity, is not found in our brain, but rather in the electromagnetic field of this organ. "Consciousness is the experience of nerves connecting to the brain's self-generated electromag-

netic field to guide what we call 'free will' and our voluntary actions," McFadden said. (La Nación, 2020, s.p.)

If proven, this developing theory could mean the answer to many of the questions currently being formulated from the vast field of neurosciences, since it would mean that the electromagnetic energy contained in the brain has a still unexplored potential, useful for the growth of several fields, mainly neurological, psychological or medical.

Now, moving on to another aspect of consciousness, from the "moral" side, the truth is that today more and more societies have been corrupting at a frankly alarming rate; values, ethics, have fallen into disuse in the face of the authorities' indifference, who far from worrying or focusing efforts to balance the series of injustices of which minorities are victims daily, seem to protect corrupt subjects and even extol or reward their superior behavior over the rest of the population:

There is added suffering to what we are experiencing such as corruption, political malpractice, evictions, financial market abuses and that long list not only impoverishes our living conditions, already based on pure survival, but also impoverishes the sense of our humanity. What aggravates the situation is that no one comes out and says, "I'm sorry." What makes our spirits worse is there is not a soul that is ashamed of what it has done or allowed to happen, knowing its consequences. The thing that damages our human sense is some hearts have not suffered pain due to the anguish of others, nor the slightest guilt for their irresponsibility, nor the inflammation necessary to jointly assume part of the burden and the solution to so many problems. (El País, 2016B, s.p.)

The justice system fails, the security system, of course; the authority and the group of individuals who work side by side to establish more severe sanctions, and just, prolonged, and strict sentences. In addition, it highlights the scarcity of well-founded values that can be enriched or rewarded to force the corrupt, criminals and anyone who acts to the detriment of social good with the sole purpose of exalting their own: "Every action arises from an intention that, however interested it may be for oneself, will have repercussions on others and the world. From there is born the moral conscience that seeks to distinguish between the principles that govern oneself and the ethical consideration of his actions" (El País, 2016B, s. p.).

Mainly in Latin America, corruption is consistently among the first positions in the indices or indicators, since its core is precisely in the bodies or institutions that govern nations. The most corrupt or perverse individuals hide among the ranks of its staff, who prevent reforms, proposals, or initiatives for change, and an effective cleaning that ends the daily emergence of new corrupts driven by the need for a better salary to support their families or promote/maintain their lifestyle.

One of the most recognized indices of corruption percentages is the one prepared by the agency called Transparency International (TI). The graph shown below shows the place occupied by the main Latin American countries:

Graph 1
Average CPI for Latin American countries 2012-2015

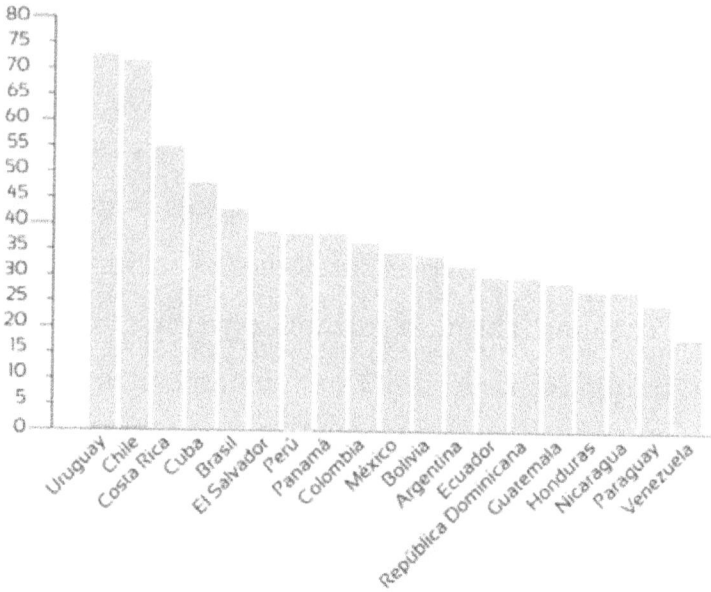

Source: Vásquez (2018).

Internationally, Mexico, for example, is located almost in the middle of the statistics, very close to Bolivia and Argentina; however, as the Vásquez study progresses, in terms of public security aspects, payment of bribes, and justice administration, it rises in all the graphs to the first five positions or the first.

What is the relationship of this work with the

research topic? Well, it is the link between the lack of conscience and corruption, which brings to light many more problems that rot society every day, such as those thrown by Vásquez's graphs.

Neurosciences strive to show how it is possible to condition the brain for better or for worse, hence, if you want to stop the type of indicated corrupt behavior, you must act, first, from education, from positive reinforcement, and act in congruence with what is preached and, above all, with what is believed. It is increasingly difficult to find good arguments to impart values or educate conscience if one witnesses daily how impunity, indifference, and corruption are gaining ground, passing by before the authorities:

> The times of tribulations are optimal for pessimism and parasitism. The consideration that the world is sinking and has no solution gains followers immersed in the moral feelings expressed by P. F. Strawson: resentment, indignation, and guilt. All of them are manifested in our interpersonal relationships, which, ultimately, determine the very meaning of our social behavior. Perhaps there is a glimpse

of something that does not allude so much to moral duties and obligations as to sensitivities. (El País, 2016B, s. p.)

It is imperative to start with the change in the individualistic mentality to transform it into a team one. Education is a key pillar, extremely valuable if we talk about modifications regarding codes of conduct at a mental level.

The brain learns everything that the individual repeats and does consciously; therefore, it adapts in order to protect itself, to ensure the subsistence of the individual. With the correct stimuli, consciousness is capable of learning or developing mechanisms to improve its perceptions, and abilities, and turn them into favorable ones for its own growth and that of its peers.

Vásquez (2018) states in his research that one of the most associated factors with corruption incidence is poverty because due to the limitations of certain population sectors to access decent housing, the basic food basket, health services or medicines, a decent or quality education, is that the way of "easy" access to money or the desire for power that crime grants, bad influences, derive in the corruption of individuals to satisfy all your goals, personal urgencies or for the benefit of your loved ones:

> However, moderate poverty has been increasing, as well as poverty in general. This is because the main engine to get out of poverty is to have a formal job that includes a living wage, and it is on this point that Mexico has not made progress. For this reason, no matter how wise the government action seems to be in reducing social deprivations, the main generator of poverty remains: the absence of well-paid formal jobs. (Vásquez, 2018, pp. 162-163)

In this way, the author concludes that if the levels of impunity, which he considers to be guilty of the increase in corruption, were eradicated, the situation regarding this evil would improve considerably, since the penalties, sanctions or punishments would have a real effect as first determining measure of correction for corrupt sectors: "To the extent that the violation of human rights is a problem that requires technical solutions related to government action, if it is possible to influence these explanatory variables, it will be possible to have a greater exercise of political rights" (Vásquez, 2018, p. 173).

Faced with the maelstrom of evil unleashed by corruption, conscience will always be an ally, for better or worse, of each individual, depending on the type of purpose or job that is desired to be granted. In the midst of a time when limits, values, ethics, morality are so scarce and little appreciated, education must prevail, in addition to the energetic impulse regarding behaviors that benefit a reflective thought oriented towards the common good, without forgetting your own or focused on efficient teamwork.

The role of neurosciences, always in collaboration with sister disciplines, is essential because it shows the human being an alternative to get to know himself better, as it opens a window into his own interior, making an x-ray of each aspect that makes up his psyche, discovering functions, reactions, perceptive stimuli for each emotion experienced, making the approach to the entire universe that encloses the mind much more transparent and affordable, as well as the neural advantages and disadvantages of violating social codes by harming third parties in search of their own benefit.

Conscience is what determines if the moral conduct of each person is valuable or not, and how it is possible to train it, as if it were a muscle. For this, it requires cerebral education and specific neural interrelationships, such as those analyzed in Chapter II. Each awareness-raising motivates change and is the beginning of a more humanistic path, in which human dignity is the main value and is oriented towards personal development and social transformation.

Conscience is the mirror that reflects our actions. Mirrors reflect what appears, without value judgments, whether the reflection is good or bad, beautiful or ugly. The existence of consciousness is shown to each individual in the form in which it is. It is an echo of one's own being.

This is how conscience becomes a categorical imperative of hope for the survival of human life.

We can affirm the scientific study of consciousness through neurosciences does not eliminate humanist values, rather reinforcements, since neurons can have a causal force.

It is the cause of life and the purpose of life that defines the conscious choices we cling to in this awakening.

The real deal is waking up. Once we are aware, everything returns to its place. Balance.

This consciousness is possible if we return to the origin, to the nature of all things.

CONCLUSION

Goethe affirmed that we cannot extract the pattern of our actions from an abstract law mysteriously located over our heads, but only from personal and irreversible decisions in the roaring bosom of history.

Corruption continues to rise as a power structure that permeates different areas. It is not only an ideological question or a structural question of society. Today, neurosciences warn that corruption involves a stimulated neural mechanism that leads to absolute confidence of the corrupt in the impunity of his acts. It is that impunity that corrodes power itself.

Sameness is inherent in power. The absolute character of power, in this case, represents an absolute immunity to sanction, in the first instance, the self-sanction that the corrupt should have if he did not have the alerts of his brain system asleep.

The alerts of the cerebral system must also be located in each person in society, and must be much stronger in those people who represent and are part of the control organisms; there must be a social reaction of punishment and rejection, generated by the neural mechanisms of each subject. This, in turn, requires deep brain exercise. It must be a constant decision of all people to promote a world free of corruption. Unfortunately, the social distrust in justice and its law have been *in crescendo*.

The victims of corruption —society— disappear in judicial practice. Being blurred, the right to punishment and the right to recover what was stolen vanishes; the victims tend to generate a cerebral mechanism of disinterest since the ethics of the judicial system are also blurred in the face of this epidemic.

It is imperative to take plural, joint and simultaneous measures that aim to dismantle corruption as a model of power, especially with an awareness of the commitment to the guarantee-right relationship of the victims of corruption; because, when the sanction does not exist, the impunity of the corrupt is sustained.

Being corrupt is a decision; the right to freedom matters, the very essence of free will. However, the responsibility to act freely implies that a person must always do what he considers right. The real problem for a corrupt brain is for it to determine if it is right to break the law.

There is a position that indicates the theory of acts would be flawed according to the advanced approach of neuroscience. Pivoting on this premise reduces the responsibility of a person's actions when he commits an act of corruption.

The corrupt act is a human act, and human acts are the consequences of neural networks and how we train our brains.

Borges identified in his stories — "The circular ruins", and "The secret miracle" — that what is in the mind of a person is in the universe; and the physicist Jean Pierre Garnier Malet, with his theory of quantum doubling, has been able to demonstrate it; therefore, I maintain that we create reality.

The absolute understanding of the functioning of the brain is still in its infancy because this is a universe in itself. Our mind and brain store information to authorize it by keeping it in a corner of our brain structures.

There is a store of information as something innate to the human being. Carl Jung called it the collective unconscious, something like a universal library of wisdom. The entire universe is like living matter, and Jung held that all life has an unconscious.

All humanity shares information from the unconscious as a kind of psychic inheritance. In this sense, Jung's collective unconscious proposes to recognize that there is no person who develops in isolation and separated from the envelope called society, that is why individual acts affect both collectively, whether they are negative such as corruption or positive such as empathy.

Furthermore, we are a perfect holistic system. When an attempt is made to divide the brain system between emotion and reason, a break is generated in the purpose of that uniqueness: integrity as a human being.

Neurosciences shed light on what was understood as the triune brain, which was expressed in three brain systems; reptilian, as the basis of the first brain evolution, where we find impulses and instinctive reactions. As a second cerebral evolution, explains Dr. Paul Maclean in *The Tribune Brain in Evolution* (1990), we have the limbic or mammalian system in which emotions emerge, and conditions behavior. Finally, the neocortex, responsible for logic and rational thought, exercises the brain's most complex.

We do not behave like robots, so we cannot fall into the mistake of believing that we are only impulsive, automatic, and intuitive; or, even worse, that there is a divorce between reason and emotion.

Likewise, those who maintain that the brain is divided, whether in emotion-reason or in a triune brain, move away from the new neuroscientific understanding, in which the bases and structures of the brain are those that define the behavior of a person by the brain connections that produce and by the whole of its brain organ. Moreover, the acts of corruption require the alteration of a determined and sustained cerebral gear, because the numbness of the emotional and rational alerts of the corrupt person occurs over time. In that synchrony, the weight of moral issues is not innocuous.

In this instance, the possibility of identifying the structure of a corrupt person in relation to neurosciences is based on parrhesia, strictly on ethically based moral responsibility.

For this reason, the law is a guarantee for the fulfill-ment of the moral responsibilities that men have, and they are the judges who solve moral problems with legal tools.

The ethical basis matters to turn the tables and promote the attitudes that make it possible in a differ-ent world. Ethics serves to remember that it is an invest-ment to save suffering by doing what is possible in our power to do. This branch also supposes the generation of a virtuous circle. Ethics should be our humanist end.

There is no trust without a perception of ethical responsibility and, in the absence of trust, what exists is a mere guarantee; where this dimension goes through, it does so with flawed and improper activities. Corrup-tion represents the ultimate betrayal of public and indi-vidual trust.

Inexorably among the most fervent desires of the people is the reorganization of the social system, more inclusive, more empathetic, where primarily there is awareness of the acts. We will reach a point where the laws, at least those that determine what is essential, will be known and conscious by all. You don't discover America twice.

In the legal system, acts of corruption are analyzed for each act. The attributes of legal acts are understood as free from external biases, intentional, and with full discernment.

In order to sustain this legal presumption as a principle, we must descend to the bases of conscience, as that constant return to oneself, of ethical confrontation of one's own being and as an essentially moral phenomenon. Conscience is the bearer of the moral mandate.

It is in consciousness, where we reach intellectual maturity of understanding of our actions, and we give value to the consequences of them; where we can determine and discern what is right, what is wrong, and what essential human limits we should not cross.

In it, the intention is born as a purpose of conduct, with a reflective design to act correctly, to produce an effect, for something to happen; that is, giving meaning and reference for significant compliance.

And it is, in the conscience, where responsibility is born, where each person assumes the life that he chooses to have because it is there where the true exercise of freedom prevails.

Freedom is where human beings exist authentically and recognize their own identity through free decisions and actions.

"Man is condemned to be free."
JEAN PAUL SARTRE

ABOUT THE AUTHOR

CYNTHIA CASTRO is a lawyer, owner and reference of Castro & Bordier Law Firm in the city of Comodoro Rivadavia, Province of Chubut, Argentina.

She is a graduate of the Blas Pascal University of Córdoba Capital, Argentina and in addition to her basic degree, she has obtained several diplomas related to law and five master's degrees awarded by Argentine Universities and Institutes dependent on European Universities. These include a master's degree in Psychopathology and Neuroscience at the Miguel de Cervantes University in Spain.

As a speaker, she has participated in several International Congresses in America, including the First Ibero-American Congress of Constitutional Law at the University of Buenos Aires (UBA).

She is passionate about psychology, physics, philosophy, and mathematics.

She has volunteered in Nairobi, Kenya for the human rights of children, orphans, and war refugees in Southern Africa.

Furthermore, she has written legal and neuroscience articles for the specialized law journal Microjuris.

Castro was born and grew up throughout her childhood and adolescence in the city of Comodoro Rivadavia in Patagonia, Argentina.

In her spare time, she plays the violin, writes, reads, paints, and trains physically and mentally in the belief that soul, body, and spirit are one; she likes winter sports, enjoys the summer wherever she is, and considers herself a "citizen of the world" she enjoys traveling when her commitments allow it.

CONTACT INFORMATION

E-MAIL:
info@cyncastro.com

WHATSAPP:
+54 9 297 472 1045

FACEBOOK
@dracynthiacastro

INSTAGRAM
@dracynthiacastro

TWITTER
@dracyncastro

ESTUDIO JURÍDICO CASTRO & BORDIER:
Instagram: @estudio_castrobordier

THANKS FOR READING!
WE HOPE YOU ENJOYED
THIS BOOK

The Author reads every comment posted on her Amazon page.

We would appreciate it if you shared your opinion about this work, as this will help other readers to make their own decisions to invest their own time and resources in this content.

Two things before you leave your comment:

First, we ask for only frank feedback, reflecting the true impact this book has had on you.

Second, that these comments are practical with the intention of helping others make their own decisions.

If you've enjoyed this book and want to share your thoughts with the Author as well as future readers, we'd love for you to leave a review on its Amazon page (just look for the title on the search bar).

Your comments and star rating will help others discover the Author's message and know what to expect

Thank you for your support!

EDITORIAL MISIÓN

REFERENCES

Bertone, M. (2018). El cerebro corrupto. [BLOG]. Available in: https://bincaglobal.org/why-you-should-read-every-day/

Cavada, C. (2017). "Historia de la Neurociencia" en *Sociedad Española de Neurociencia* [BLOG]. Available in: https://www.senc.es/introduccion-historica-a-la-neurociencia/

Diario *El País* (2016). *El cerebro corrupto.* [BLOG]. Available in: https://elpais.com/elpais/2016/05/03/ciencia/1462289605_959427.html

Diario El País (2016B). *Necesitamos conciencia moral.* Available in: https://elpais.com/elpais/2013/05/30/eps/1369936183_707211.html

Fernández C. F. (2020). "Así funciona el cerebro de una

persona corrupta" en *El Tiempo* [BLOG]. Available in: https://www.eltiempo.com/salud/como-funciona-el-cerebro-de-una-persona-corrupta-457922

Figueroa, G. (2013). "Las ambiciones de la neuroética: fundar científicamente la moral" in *Acta Bioethica*, vol. 19, núm. 2, Chile: Universidad de Valparaíso.

García García, E. (2017). "Neurociencia y ética: La Neuroética" in *Pesquisas*, vol. 1, núm. 3, Madrid: Universidad Complutense.

Huerta, E. (2016). "¿Cómo funciona el cerebro de los corruptos? Esto dice la ciencia" en *El Comercio* [BLOG]. Available in: https://elcomercio.pe/tecnologia/ciencias/funciona-cerebro-corruptos-esto-dice-ciencia-noticia-506186-noticia/?ref=ecr

La Información. (2016). *Así actúa el cerebro de un corrupto al cometer una estafa o aceptar un soborno* [BLOG]. Available in: https://www.lainformacion.com/tecnologia/cerebro-corrupto-comete-aceptasoborno_0_950905944.html/

La Nación (2020). *Una nueva teoría sugiere que la conciencia no se encuentra ubicada en el cerebro.* Available in: https://www.lanacion.com.ar/lifestyle/una-nueva-teoria-sugiere-conciencia-no-se-nid2496614/

León-Domínguez U. y León-Carrión J. (2019) "Modelo neurofuncional de la conciencia: bases neurofisiológicas y cognitivas" in *Revista de Neurología*, vol. 69, núm. 4.

Meza, D. (2018). "La ciencia detrás de la corrupción: ¿qué pasa en el cerebro de un corrupto?" in *La crónica del Quindío* [BLOG]. Available in: https://www.cronicadelquindio.com/noticias/ciencia-y-tecnologia/la-ciencia-detrs-de-la-corrupcin-qu-pasa-en-el-cerebro-de-un-corrupto

Morgado Bernal, I. (2014). "¿Qué es la conciencia?, ¿Cómo la crea el cerebro?" en *Investigación y ciencia* [BLOG]. Disponible en: https://www.investigacionyciencia.es/blogs.p.sicologia-y-neurociencia/37/posts/qu-es-la-consciencia-cmo-la-crea-el-cerebro-18107

Moscote Salazar, L. R. (2018). "El cerebro carcomido del corrupto: del acto inmoral a la aceptación social" en *Al Poniente* [BLOG]. Available in: https://alponiente.com/el-cerebro-carcomido-del-corrupto-del-acto-inmoral-a-la-aceptacion-social/

Nature (2021). "Descifrando la neurociencia de la

consciencia" en *UNAM Global* [BLOG]. Available in: https://unamglobal.unam.mx/descifrando-la-neurociencia-de-la-consciencia/

Orellana Rodríguez, V. y De Antonio Hernández, E. (2018). "Así funciona la mente de un corrupto" en *El Economista*. Disponible en: https://www.eleconomista.es/opinion-blogs/noticias/9513609/11/18/Asi-funciona-la-mente-de-un-corrupto.html

Ramírez Palma, G.; Sánchez Gonzáles, H.; Tovar Tovar, E. N. y Zapata Islas, L. A. (2014). "La corrupción ¿un proceso adaptativo? Un enfoque neuropsiquiátrico" in *Educación y Salud*, México: Universidad del Estado de Hidalgo. Available in: https://www.uaeh.edu.mx/scige/boletin/icsa/n5/e11.html

Romero, F. R.; Mansilla Olivares, A. y Rivera Cruz, A. (2019). *Neurofisiología para estudiantes de Medicina*, México: UNAM.

Sociedad Española de Neurología (2021). "¿Qué es la Neurología?" en *Sociedad Española de Neurociencia* [BLOG]. Available in: https://www.sen.es/

Tirapu Ustárroz, J. y Goñi Sáez, F. (2016). "El problema cerebro-mente: sobre la conciencia." en *Neurología.com Revista de Neurología/Formación online*.

Available in: https://neurologia.com/noticia/5824/
el-problema-cerebro-mente-sobre-la-conciencia

Vásquez, L. D. (2018). "Derechos Humanos y corrupción en México: una radiografía" in *Impacto de la corrupción en los Derechos Humanos*. México: Instituto de Estudios Constitucionales del Estado de Querétaro.

Vélez, M. (2019). "Breve historia de la neurociencia" in *La Mente es Maravillosa* [BLOG]. Available in: https://lamenteesmaravillosa.com/breve-historia-de-la-neurociencia/

Zumalabe Makirriain, J. M. (2016). "El estudio neurológico de la conciencia: Una valoración crítica" in *Anales de Psicología*, vol. 32, núm. 1, Murcia: Universidad del País Vasco/Euskal Herriko Unibertsitatea.

www.ingramcontent.com/pod-product-compliance
Lightning Source LLC
Chambersburg PA
CBHW071029280326
41935CB00011B/1506